T0114971

Like A Bridge Over Troubled Water:

An Ethnography on Strategies of Bodily Navigation of Male Refugees in Cape Town

Leah Davina Junck

Langaa Research & Publishing CIG
Mankon, Bamenda

Publisher

Langaa RPCIG
Langaa Research & Publishing Common Initiative Group
P.O. Box 902 Mankon
Bamenda
North West Region
Cameroon
Langaagrp@gmail.com
www.langaa-rpcig.net

Distributed in and outside N. America by African Books Collective
orders@africanbookscollective.com
www.africanbookscollective.com

ISBN-10: 9956-550-01-9

ISBN-13: 978-9956-550-01-2

Table of Contents

Chapter 6
Dream until your dreams come true?
On bodily mappings of self

Acknowledgements

This book would not have come into being without the seven men I was working with, Sam, Matthew, Scott, Miguel, Daniel, Issa and Shawn.[1]. The support and encouragement of my supervisor, Dr Divine Fuh, was also essential in materialising this research. I owe them all thanks and am grateful for the time and efforts invested in this work by them. To me, it was a time of discovery in many ways – regarding myself and others – and I want it to be known how meaningful and precious the process was to me. I also want to express my gratitude to SWEAT and Dr Gordon Isaacs in particular, who invited me to attend meetings and thus offered me the opportunity to meet my informants through the organisation. I felt warmly welcomed and free to carry out the research in ways I deemed appropriate. My gratitude shall also be expressed to Dr Francis Nyamnjoh, who encouraged me to publish this piece of writing and who offers great inspiration through his own works and insights.

---

[1] All synonyms.

About this book

Juristically and socially, the refugee body is seen as easy to categorize, move, manage and dispose of. This book is based on a qualitative, in-depth ethnographic study and seeks to outlines the strategies employed by male refugees in navigating their daily lives within different social landscapes of Cape Town, in spite of being neatly objectified as 'foreign' and the grim precarities (in the sense of Butler's framing of the term, 2016) resulting from this objectification. It grapples with the question of how the men manage to bring about certainty in the face of multiple uncertainties and extends its focus to the men's dreams and the modes by which these are sought to be achieved in the face of unpredictability.

The reader of this ethnography may interpret the outlined findings in the context of current global politics in which different brands of apocalyptic nationalism, expressed through machismo as a political style, wall-building and xenophobia, are in vogue and respond to nation states having, to some degree, lost their influence over human circumstance. Reported 'floods' of immigrants that fall within this rhetoric of machismo fuel notions of there being a competition to stay 'socially alive' (see Biehl, 2007) and the media's attention span on brutal and often lethal attacks on foreigners of African origin is often short-lived in South Africa. Notions of African 'outsiders' as being demanding, unwelcome intruders (see Harris, 2002; Nyamnjoh, 2006; Gordon, 2016) are revived and manifested through 'public memory' (see Appadurai, 2003) and social interaction. What is more, the (poor) black, male body more broadly has been constructed as dangerous and suspicious (Oliver, 2003; Posel, 2005) and remains vigorously controlled and policed in the post-apartheid context. What Sichone (2008) has called 'independent economic migrants' who create a life largely independently from labour contracts and visas manage to venture beyond various confines of nation states and re-define themselves in the process. Against this backdrop, exploring the experiences of men seeking refuge in Cape Town (a city associated with beauty, affluence and opportunities) becomes a fascinating, complex and necessary task at hand.

In my interviews with seven male refugees from different African countries over a period of 10 weeks, I found the male refugee body and the men's bodily strategies in navigating the city to serve as a metaphorical 'bridge over troubled water'[2], rendering living possible in spaces and situations that fundamentally challenge the men's dignity and their very existence. Their life histories revealed to me that the men's bodies are in an urgent state of having to be physically maintained as the lives they lead require constant alertness and readiness to dodge the metaphorical blows handed down to them. Said bodies are also in a constant state of transition. This book intends to render apparent the men's struggles and predicaments whilst also indicating their pleasures and yearnings. The focus on bodies serves to highlight the objectification of male refugees and encourages an understanding of the experiential aspects of the men's lives. Overall, male refugees in Cape Town are revealed as capable of reclaiming the humanness they are often denied, rendering them able of a simultaneous 'suffering and smiling' (see Chabal, 2009) in the midst of precarity.

While the data for this book was collected in the winter of

---

[2] Song title, Simon and Garfunkel.

2014, just recently a reminder of the issues my informants faced on an everyday basis reached to the very core of my body. I was on the start line of the Argus, the biggest cycling race in the world, which draws thousands of internationals to the city for a collective 'fun ride' every year. Enthusiastically waiting at the Cape Town Parade to the sound of Midnight Oil's 'beds are burning', a song about forced removal and land rights in New Zealand, my group got the signal to start. Cheered on by a crowd of people, we turned onto the freeway M3 (closed for other traffic on our account) and immediately drove past temporary shelters to our right - and on towards Muizenburg and the beautiful Chapman's Peak mountain range. By the time I crossed the finish line at the Sea Point stadium, the disquieting feeling rooted in the contrasts of fun, excitement and costly entertainment right alongside niche existences and destitute conditions had, almost as a matter of course, calmly and quietly settled into my anatomy. However, the experience did serve as a corporeal reminder that, even though the view of it may be despised by many who live and buzz in the city, humans huddled under plastic covers and worn blankets on the side of the city's roads appear to be too much part of the social landscape in order to raise lasting public concern or questions about the individual, lived stories that are arduously sought to be safely sheltered.

Chapter 1

Male refugees in Cape Town

Dreaming precariously

This ethnography engages with male refugees who frequently get together in group-meetings in suburban Cape Town. The meetings are organised and moderated by the non-profit organisation SWEAT (Sex Workers Education and Advocacy Task Force), offering a space in which the men can discuss their experiences and receive legal and health advice.

A variety of precarities may limit foreign, male sex workers in their capacity to dream. This manifests in the men's objectification as refugees (linked to their juristic status as well as bodily markers) and a fragmentation of their bodies along different axes in varying contexts. However, as other ethnographies have shown (see Gondola, 1999; Jensen, 2008, Ross, 2005 and Salo, 2006; 2010; 2013), even in contexts of severe poverty and limited social visibility, visions and ideals may become deeply embodied guidelines to living a respectable life and a validated social identity. Against the backdrop of the unequal distribution of violence against refugees and their social exclusion in Cape Town, I will look at strategies of survival, as well as the practice of dreaming as counteractions to structural limitations and show that people find ways to smile in the midst of precarity and suffering, as suggested by Chabal (2009).

I am drawing on the ongoing life stories of a group of male refugees I met through SWEAT in order to emphasise the uniqueness and resilience[3] of characters who insist on having a say in navigating the course of their lives. 'Like a bridge over troubled water', the men's bodies and bodily strategies of navigation help to traverse precarity in different social spaces in Cape Town in a continuous process of becoming. These strategies, although mainly centred on the men's bodies, are used not just in order to survive, but also to stabilise their lives in imaginative ways. I shall therefore also focus on the imaginative worlds that lie beyond the immediate use of the body as a survival tool. 'Dreaming' in this ethnography serves as an agentive concept in emphasising the ways in which oppressive structures are resisted and in outlining the complexities that lie within hoping and desiring notwithstanding dwindling opportunities.

Through this particular lens, I seek to engage with Emirbayer and Mische's (1998) framing of agency as not only the capacity for action, but also imagination as an agency for action, which is socially unequally distributed (see Appadurai, 2003). Thereby, I intend to illuminate the ways in which my informants manoeuvre and make living possible in spaces in which they are considered to be 'socially dead' (Biehl, 2007) in the sense that they live the pervasive lives of 'ex-humans' (Biehl, 2007) and are denied social exchanges that nurture humanness. The 'public deaths' (Biehl, 2007) or unrecognised lives (Butler, 2016) are consequences of both, being identified as an African foreigner and a sex worker and legitimate frameworks that force male refugees into 'zones of social abandonment' (Biehl, 2007).

Chapter 1 interrogates mentioned strategies employed by male refugees in Cape Town in maintaining their bodies and

---

[3] See Obrist's (2006) account on living successfully with urban risks.

stabilising their lives by focusing on immediate needs. Bodies play an important role in what Lévi-Strauss (1966) has called 'bricolage', making do with what is at hand. Due to the extreme scarcity of resources available to the men, their bodies are used as primary tools in engaging with problems as well as opportunities. Their corporeal existence and engagements with others in different spaces become relevant in interpreting their subtle forms of resistance to domination, enabling them to reclaim autonomy from all-pervasive forces of culture, economics and politics (see De Certeau 2014 on strategies of resistance).

Chapter 2 aims to reveal the body in the process of becoming and how it is used to dream with. I conceptualise the men's visions for the future as 'selfscape dreams' (Hollan, 2014) or maps of the self, which come into being through an interplay of memory, present experience, as well as imagination (in line with Emirbayer and Mische's [1998] understanding of action being informed by the past, but also oriented toward the future and the present). Since the body comprises of both, the biological and imaginative, subconscious awareness and desires are just as important to consider as the physical engagement with the world on an everyday basis. In looking at the men's corporeality (Csordas, 1999), their notion of being in a body and oriented in space, I am going to engage with both aspects without treating them as dichotomous. By addressing survival strategies and dreams as agentive forms of productive escapism, I hope to bring to the fore the various ways in which people re-make space and reclaim humanness and forms of citizenship in precarious contexts in which they are conceptualised as lesser (see Allison, 2012; Butler, 2016; Standing, 2011; Stewart, 2012) or 'ex-human' (Biehl, 2007).

Rendered 'foreign'

As I have touched upon, male refugees in Cape Town are limited in their actions on different levels because they are exposed to great risks as foreigners (see Nyamnjoh, 2006; Harris, 2002; Gordon, 2016). They also may, in some ways, not fit into the 'hegemonic ideal' of a powerful man (Cornwall, 2000; Gutmann, 1997; Seale, 2009). Dominant (but relative) societal discourses regarding masculinity, which, in a neoliberal context, are often linked to a capacity to spend money, create great pressure for male refugees who are engaging in sex work as a survival strategy – as does a moral economy anchored in reproductive heterosexuality (Salo, 2010). Xenophobic attacks in recent years – often lethal and destructive on many levels – have captured the attention of the media only fleetingly. African men foreign to a metropolis are also often part of an economy that is invisible to many (see Ndjio, 2006), which renders the ways in which selves are understood in this context an interesting focal point.

Social studies on male refugees in Cape Town have not been established as a field of interest and public statements on refugees are often sweeping and condemning[4]. Due to refugees

---

[4] This is suggested by an article published on IRIN (linked to the UN office) in 2012 (http://www.irinnews.org/report/88303/south-africa-police-blame-illegal-immigrants-for-crime). Limpopo chief of police, Calvin Sengani, stated that the province, which borders Zimbabwe, had to deal with foreign nationals 'flooding our towns and cities. They cause a great number of problems with crime; we arrest them and protect them with resources that are intended for our citizens.' Gauteng's former police chief, Simon Mpembe, claimed that Gauteng was home to as many as three million 'illegal' immigrants who have to be extensively and expensively policed. Landau (director of the University of the Witwatersrand's Forced Migration Studies Programme) responded that the claim that undocumented foreign nationals were responsible for one of the world's

4

being limited in their visibility and audibility (as argued in this ethnography) and a lack of existing research, what is known about this cohort can be described as imaginative and wholesale, to say the least. As one of the few authors engaging with the topic, Sharp (2008) has argued that the construction of non-South Africans of African origin as 'outsiders' is welcomed by the elites in their efforts to distract from the gulf between 'haves' and 'have-nots' and in keeping the public discourse focused on tensions within the latter group. In the grander scheme of things, Sichone (2008) has described such divisions as 'global apartheid', policed by a regime of passports and visas, which can be easily recognised as replicating colonial patterns and still doing the job of keeping wealth and poverty effectively apart (Sichone, 2008). As a part of what Standing (2011) has called the 'precariat', refugees become not only vulnerable to extreme exploitation from the higher social classes, but also to attacks from within the precariat. This is due to their lack of a political voice and access to secure wage labour, as well as their status as non-citizens or what Standing (2011) has referred to as 'denizens'.

At first glance, the men I interviewed seem to be socially excluded on any conceivable level with their lives being led on the periphery of urban areas and in dependence on a recycling economy. With xenophobia in South Africa constituting a violent practice rather than an attitude (Harris, 2002), physical threats have found their ways into the archives in the form of newspaper articles (Harris, 2002) and have thereby integrated the separateness of African 'foreigners' as a homogeneous group into the 'public memory'[5].

---

highest crime rates was not based on statistics.

[5] The archive of public memory is a concept used by Appadurai (2003).

Sex work and SWEAT in South Africa

Although there have been movements and motions in South Africa to decriminalise sex work since the 1990s and the ruling party ANC has expressed its support of such efforts (Wojcicki, 2003), to date, sex work remains a punishable offence according to South African law (Act 23 of 1957). Sex workers in South Africa are vulnerable to customer abuse, police brutality (Massawe and Kueppers, 2010) and intimate partner violence (Gorven, 2014). Uncertainties and violence with regards to authorities and hesitance to consult social and health services result in health risks, lack of legal recognition, access grants and other basic services for individuals engaging in sex work (Pudifin and Bosch 2012). Due to their social status, refugee sex workers are even less likely to reach out for help. Whilst refugees in South Africa show a significant burden of mental distress, linked to the challenges of living in an often hostile context (Idemudia, 2017; Thela et al., 2017), xenophobia is also deeply entrenched in the South African public health system (Crush and Tawodzera, 2014), rendering spaces intended for support just another hostile environment.

Perpetuating the mistreatment of sex workers are discourses on sex work framed around discussions on morality, which are often informed by a religious rhetoric (Pudifin and Bosch, 2012) and notions of sex workers being 'unclean' (Ackermann and de Klerk, 2002). Likewise do notions that sex workers put themselves in dangerous situations where rape can be expected (Brown, Duby and Bekker, 2012) and beliefs that sex workers cannot be sexually violated in principal (Pauw and Brener, 2003) contribute to the dehumanizing treatment of people of the profession. Yet, limited qualitative studies capture experiences and resilience in the context of transactional sex, especially in the global South (see Wojcicki, 2001; Jewkes et al., 2012; Vickerman, 2013; Mamabolo, 2017) and even less so with regards to male sex workers.

I was introduced to my informants through the organisation SWEAT, which promotes the political recognition of sex work as work, which would likely lead to much safer working conditions (Shannon et al., 2015). In the long run, SWEAT wants to eliminate the stigma[6] attached to sex work and thus the frequent attacks[7] on sex workers. Political long-term goals are supplemented with different groups and programmes of different sizes and durations, based on the premise of peer- education, through which conversations and exchanges are stirred. The groups are often organised around issues of health but also address other topics, such as safety, dealing with the police, and avoiding or handling conflicts with their clients.

Doing research in Cape Town

Spaces are never neutral, nor do they carry the same meanings, opportunities and temporalities. Banks (2011), for instance, argues that spaces can be deeply stigmatised. This applies to townships as well as to 'untraditional' sleeping spots such as parks and fields in the city core, sheltered from the common (or at least the privileged) eye. The men come to Cape Town (most of them after having stayed in Johannesburg) expecting a flourishing, tourism-industry stimulated economy

---

[6] Literature dealing with sex work in South Africa particularly tends to focus on disease and violence and thus perpetuate the stigma of sex workers as containers and distributors of moral ills.

[7] Via social media (such as Facebook) SWEAT takes note of the frequent cases of violent deaths of sex workers.

in Cape Town. However, what (Tucker, 2009:49) has referred to as South Africa's 'Reigning Queen' when it comes to sex tourism, flourishes only some months of the year, as do other types of tourist entertainment. The men generate their income through a mix of practices, depending on the kind of the opportunities that arise. More often than not, the men wind up doing intense labour for much less than the street-market value of it.

'Cities, like nations', Sanderock (2003:33) has argued, 'keep their shape by moulding their citizens'. In coming to Cape Town and in the process of remaking place, the men become moulded into 'disposable labourers' (Standing, 2011). This becomes particularly challenging as they constantly move between different spaces imbued with different temporalities and meanings. Sam, for instance, had a job as a waiter in the Waterfront and tried to go back to Philippi but often ended up sleeping outdoors in town with his brother Matthew.

The different meanings attached to spaces, the male refugee body occupying them, and the socialites possible within them inform the men's corporeality which is continuously re-made, as is the meaning of space and sense of self. Being a refugee and made into a body that signifies non-belonging and triggers suspicion in the South African context, 'dream on!' is an irony-heavy, dismissive message that is received on a daily basis when refugees attempt to participate on platforms of visibility, which are reserved for the fortuitous ones who have access to security measures, health support, social and physical mobility.

Chapter 2

Troubling bodies and the mother city

Summer in the city

Cape Town in summer is bristling with movement. A synthesis of noise and smells suggests a multiplicity of possibilities and experiences. Shopping in town becomes a sweaty affair this time of the year, drawing me to the next best café for an iced coffee afterwards. Office hours feel shortened by the promise of being able to go to Muizenberg Beach and watch the surfers, before jumping into those waves myself and wash away the last bit of heaviness from my shoulders. During the summer months, the slow crowds walking the streets of Cape Town feel like a big, comfortable cocoon to me. It is as though I share an experience of the space with others without having to engage with them and expose myself to their judgment. There is a great feeling of safety inherent in this way of moving and being for me.

Comes winter, the streets suddenly seem empty. The cocoon has disappeared and whatever smells there may have been have long blown into all directions by fierce winds. The few heavily layered and coated people in the streets appear to walk faster now – this may be due to hovering dark clouds that carry the threat of cold showers, or, perhaps, a feeling of exposedness. For refugee men, looming winter translates onto a drastic intensification of their everyday precarities. While their access to social platforms of visibility is limited any time of the year, winter inhibits opportunities to move about, socialise and find income opportunities. This leaves them to hushfully hibernate, along with the tourism industries and other work they rely on, such as construction and gardening jobs. Many of the spaces used in endeavours to avoid negative attention are tolerated while camouflaged as publically 'unused' or undesirable spaces. However, shelterless people making use of public space are not only often met with despise but, are also frequently penalised for finding niches for their existence. This attitude symbolically manifests in the erection of spikes under the freeway bridge in town that leads nowhere, because the project was never completed. This purposeless space, which could have at least served as shelter from wind and rain, is thus denied to those without any assets.

The South African police, referees of societal values, often contribute to the confinement of the presence of the poor and voiceless to particular spaces, with the emptiness of the streets in winter rendering one uncomfortably visible to their vigilant eyes. I sometimes encountered the men who contributed to the ethnography walking the streets in a slightly hunched manner, carrying bags, with their faces shadowed by caps. I suspect the ways in which their bodies are carried to be related to frequent approaches by the police while they are out looking for work, food or sociality, which often leads to their arrest as suspected criminals. The men's 'trouble' is that they are not only identified as belonging to a particular class, the exploitable 'precariat' (Standing, 2011). Their papers, accents and general association with a foreign African countries shape the often hostile ways in which they are encountered by locals (see Harris, 2002; Nyamnjoh, 2006; Sichone, 2008).

Making this city work for you

What the men I was working with share, is access to the institution SWEAT, which aims to equip them with a basic knowledge of their rights and serves as a platform for the exchange of experiences and modes of manoeuvring the city safely. Most importantly, the organisation intends building up the men's self-esteem, which can be seen as a counter movement to structures that reduces the men to bodies that may be used as labour force or for sexual pleasure. Within this broader context, bodies become an essential tool in managing day-to-day life, in maintaining the men's existence – and in aspiring to a brighter future. In the following, I will elaborate on the experiential aspects of the everyday and the maintenance of the body as something of value, in spite of being stripped of a number of rights and rendered undeserving of social support. The different journeys that brought my informants to South Africa and the relationships they established in Cape Town are of great relevance as they constitute determining factors in how life itself is conceptualised and negotiated on an everyday basis. I thus want to offer a glimpse into the life stories that were shared with me as they render apparent the unique mechanisms and niches refugee men find in order to survive and live in a rather hostile environment.

I would like to emphasise that this ethnography is concerned with a particular group of individuals and does not aim to draw general conclusions with regards to sex work – nor does it intend to render experiences of all male refugees universal. Instead, it focuses on specific experiences of foreign men, who share the commonality of living precarious lives and knowing about the organisation SWEAT and the different forms of support it. Sex work as practised by the men is seen as a way of surviving, rather than a profession, which is not to say that the majority of street sex-workers feel this way.

Being a foreign male becomes a highly relevant factor, especially when opportunities for money cease and it becomes clear that there is insufficient support in place to guide the men through a rough patch. As rough patches are not a rarity, most of them live in the city shelterlessly (meaning under temporary, frequently re-located shelter or in the open) and exposed to all types of dangers to their existence. None of the men with whom I engaged could count on support from their family and seldom from friends, even though all of them locally have loosely-knit networks in place to help them manage the challenges of the everyday. Only three of my research participants were staying in townships, which are considered to be dangerous places for foreigners.

Carrying the status of a refugee limits the men's money making possibilities to a work sector that is hotly fought over by people who lack the opportunities for stable and secure work. I was witness to one of these fights when I picked up Peter at an intersection where a large crowd of men was waiting to be picked up for 'casual' work (usually in construction), which means paying very little for semi-skilled labour on a daily basis. When I slowed down, a crowd of men was quickly moving towards my car and encircled it, talking loudly across each other. Chances to be picked out of the crowd are slim if one is not to be insistent and vocal. Peter, who had asked me to pick him up at this spot, explained that he had wanted to spend the early morning hours waiting for a job opportunity before meeting me, as he would then earn more than the travel money I offered (his daily income would vary between R50 and R200, depending on the type of labour) and may be favoured over others in the future if he did a good job. This was in line with most of my informants reporting to get access to manual jobs through people they know and who are willing to recommend them as hard workers.

Most of the men were not able to keep their refugee papers 'in order' and either reported to have lost them or to have failed to extend them. When caught up in a police raid, the men usually offer a South African contact, who, either in person or over the phone, is willing to make a statement that they employ the person in question, rendering deportation less likely. Sam, a man from Zimbabwe, claims that while he was on his way home to Phillipi by train, he was asked to present his papers to the police. Seeing that his papers had long expired and the imposed R2500 fine had not been paid, he was taken to prison and kept there for the whole weekend, allegedly for the police to check his criminal record. Arrests of this kind were frequently mentioned at SWEAT, even where individuals were in possession of valid papers. While legal documents and permits in themselves carry potentials of providing access to resources, the status of being a foreigner from another African country (with or without the 'right' paperwork) likely marks a person unwanted and leads to societal exclusion.

Chapter 3

The challenged, corporeal body

Living conditions for refugees in Cape Town can be harsh and precarious. Searching for food, shelter and safety are part of the everyday existence of many refugees. This lack, blended with an exposure to xenophobia, difficulties in accessing healthcare, fragile legal statuses and conflicts with the police severely affect the bodily conditions and the corporeal existence (Csordas, 1994) of refugees in Cape Town. Engaging with these aspects, this Chapter outlines literature conceptualising bodies, dreams and resistance.

Butler (2016) describes the condition of the body as being exposed to others, pointing out its *precariousness* and vulnerability to destruction by the other. She refers to Hannah Arendt who, based on this notion, had years prior called for an investment in institutions that seek to sustain human lives and aim make them liveable, instead of regarding part of the population as socially dead, redundant or intrinsically unworthy of life and, therefore, 'ungrievable' (Butler, 2016). She states that precariousness is consequence of our social existence as bodily beings, dependent upon one another for sustenance and shelter and thus at risk of homelessness, statelessness and destitution under unjust and unequal political conditions (Butler, 2016). The political status of being a refugee means being only temporarily tolerated and only in particular spaces of society while others remain inaccessible. As aforementioned, being a refugee in South Africa also means being exposed to xenophobia (Harris, 2002; Nyamnjoh, 2006,

Sichone, 2008). These aspects render my informants (and certainly others in similar situations) vulnerable and are expression of the lack of worth ascribed to the men. While such expressions are politically induced, they deeply affect social practices. Sichone (2008) defines xenophobia as a dislike of non-nationals by nationals of a recipient state, manifesting in a violation of human rights. The status of being a non-national often leads to the affected becoming part of a reservoir of *disposable labour* (Standing, 2011).

Butler (2016) understands *precarity* to be a political issue and argues that the passions linked to our very persistence are linked to the politics of the body. Politics, she says, struggle to overcome inequalities in food distribution and rights of housing. At the same time, Butler (2016) states that precarity exposes sociality, the fragile and necessary dimensions of human interdependency and that interdependency constitutes us more than thinking beings, but indeed as social and embodied, vulnerable and passionate. Precarity as described by Butler (2016) and Allison (2012) is imbued with expectations, the consequences of their non-fulfilment, and the social ramifications this has in terms of relationships and social practices. While precarity mainly refers to the political and economic conditions under which people secure their lives, precariousness is described as a condition that is shared for human life through the exposure to others from the moment of birth and by relying on others.

The men who were sharing their stories with me explained that they did not have family in South Africa, except for two of the participants, who introduced themselves as brothers. The others stayed in infrequent contact with their families abroad and often did not feel understood by them. The social networks they established in Cape Town became essential for their everyday existence and survival. However, these relationships are not always reliable and do not necessarily provide platforms to share intimate stories and worries and receive emotional support. Some of the men said they appreciated the opportunity to talk to me and being considered worthy telling their stories, as they have grown used to being seen as potential criminals, a burden to society, hijackers of job opportunities and exploitable subjects. From their status as 'non- citizens', the men are not regarded worthy of any social support. It is therefore not only precarity that shapes their everyday lives, due to a lack of access to housing and other resources. Precariousness, a lack of social and emotional support, affects the men just as much.

If what Sharp (2000) has called *bodily integrity* is under constant attack when exposed to precariousness as defined by Butler (2016), and interdependencies are indeed social and embodied, what does this mean for men who come to Cape Town on their own and their corporeal experiences? I am going to interrogate this question by looking at the men's bodies as settings in relation to the worlds they inhabit (as Csordas, 1999, has suggested) and (as Turner 1994 has put it) as a 'material infrastructure' of the production of selves, identities and belonging. The body thus constitutes not an object, but rather is subject to culture or an existential ground for culture. An analysis of perception and practice (in the form of peoples' habitus, Bourdieu 1990) grounded in the body leads to the collapse of the conventional distinction between subject and object. Csordas builds on this, arguing that 'this collapse allows us to investigate how cultural objects (including selves) are constituted or objectified [...] in the ongoing indeterminacy and flux of adult cultural life' (1999:40). The (multiple) body-selves[8] of refugees in Cape Town become objectified and moulded into cultural objects through various perceptions, as well as practices (both their own and others) in particular ways. Exploitation and social exclusion become inscribed upon the men's bodies and selves.

As Lock (1993) has pointed out, the body, imbued with social meaning, is also historically situated, and becomes not only a signifier of belonging and order, but also an active forum for the expression of dissent and loss, thus ascribing it individual agency. She continues saying: 'These dual modes of bodily expression – belonging and dissent – are conceptualised as culturally produced and in dialectical exchange with the externalised ongoing performance of social life' (Lock, 1993:141). Refugee bodies often signify disorder and sheer lack, while they can be seen as rich *forums of expressions* in which memories of the past and everyday experiences are interpreted and negotiated. I agree with Scott (1990) when he argues that the dominant in a society never control the stage absolutely, but that their wishes normally prevail, typically generating the insults and slights to human dignity that, in turn, foster a *hidden transcript of indignation*. The everyday strategies of survival as well as the dreams of my informants can be interpreted as such 'hidden transcripts' of resistance.

This is also in line with Mbembe's notion (1992) of the body and embodiment as the playground of both, oppression and resistance. Here, hegemonic and counter-hegemonic practices, authority and subversion, power and defiance meet. Male refugees' perceptions of self and their process of becoming are, to some degree, influenced by the structural

---

[8] A term used by Van Wolputte (2004) in reference to Csordas's (1999) ideas of embodiment.

limitations the men are exposed to, such as access to social institutions of support such as housing schemes and often healthcare. However, I want to argue that this socially produced objectification of the male refugee body is not simply being reproduced by them, but that the body-self is defined in a continuous process of becoming oriented in the world through exposure to various challenges. 'Dream on!' may be a message received on a daily basis when attempting to socially participate on platforms of visibility. Nevertheless, this does not mean that this objectification remains unchallenged. In the case of the men with whom I was working, I interpreted the strategies employed in maintaining their bodies and creating stability as a form of resistance to domination (see De Certeau, 1984, on strategies and resistance). It is in this manner that the men manage to bridge the troubled water of *precarity* and *precariousness* that threaten the men's fundamental existence.

As the men experience move across different social spaces, they are exposed to processes of change and rupture. These processes, Van Wolputte (2004) points out, may often be paradoxical and evolve around experiences and understandings of time, space, self, body and identity. The self thus becomes fragmented along many axes, such as past and present or public and private. 'It is through fragmentation', Van Wolputte (2004) argues, that the sometimes violent rupture between experience and discourse can be overcome, and a sense of belonging can be achieved. Dreams can be seen as a way of achieving this sense of belonging as they offer a way to engage with the discrepancy of a body-self that is constantly being undermined and confronted with various meanings that become attached to it and carried across spaces. Multiple body images make it possible for the men to engage in a variety of contexts and relationships. Through the practice of dreaming, as I am arguing, memory and imagination form a synthesis and may, to some extent, reconcile conflicting images of the body-self.

Emirbayer and Mische (1998) frame agency as not only entailing a capacity for action, but also imagination as an agentive means for action, which is, however, socially unequally distributed (see Appadurai, 2003).This ethnography looks at the men's descriptions of a possible future as *selfscape dreams* (Hollan, 2004). Dreams and aspirations provide a map of the self's contours in the present and resonate with the engagement of the body with other objects and people in the world, across spaces and at different points in time. These kinds of dreams are related to the dreamer's current life situation and to alterations in his or her conscious and unconscious experiences self-esteem and well-being (as opposed to Freud's understanding of the latent meanings of dreams which can be deciphered through free association). In my engagement with male refugees, I regarded both biological and imaginative processes of the self as highly relevant, as engagements with the world take place on multiple levels and desires are just as much part of being oriented in the world as actual practice.

Chapter 4

Researching 'disposable bodies'

This Chapter lays out the challenges and implications of doing research on male refugee bodies in the context of an organisation that is concerned with sex work. The following is a description of the methodological paths that seemed appropriate for me to take in researching lives that are considered 'disposable' (Standing, 2011) and the ethical reflections triggered in the process of collecting and interpreting the data.

The first challenge I encountered was the recruitment of informants through SWEAT. I was invited to join a support group meeting on a Tuesday morning. I was briefly introduced to Pepsi, the new facilitator who was to organise his first meeting that day. Together we walked to an adjoined building and entered a plain room filled with school tables and chairs. The 10 men in the room had to sign up for it prior to the meeting which is a requirement for being able to attend and receive R40 travel money as well as a cup of coffee and a biscuit at each session. This is done to avoid people coming in under the pretence of doing sex work in order to access money and food, it is explained to me. When asked to introduce my research, I kept my description concise, explaining that it was concerned with the everyday life of foreign, male sex workers in Cape Town. However, throughout my fieldwork, I was repeatedly asked about particularities of the research, sometimes by the same people, which made me realise that I expected them to offer their assistance without providing sufficient information about my intentions and why I am interested in them as individuals. This realisation led me to find occasions to continue bringing up scope and purpose of the research and, at times, to discuss what I experienced as challenging in doing research. This also helped me get a better sense of the men's thoughts and of when my showing interest in the topic may be considered intrusive.

The limited time frame dedicated to the data-gathering process initially made me anxious about finding participants with whom I would be able to engage frequently, which is why I decided to offer R40 'travel money', as SWEAT does. I considered this an option mainly because I had not been able to find participants at the first meeting and, knowing that the meetings only take place every two weeks and that I would only be able to establish contact again the next time around, I wanted to make spending time with me seem more attractive and beneficial. Fuelled by these concerns, I decided to introduce my research intentions again at the 'Creative Space', a workshop offered to male sex workers (both local and foreign) every second Tuesday. When I entered the spacious, cold warehouse, my eyes moved through a sea of faces. I had not expected there to be so many people since the other group was comparably tiny. I felt my body being scanned by the men, with most eyes wandering on quickly and others seeming to linger. After everybody had settled down in the chair rows and Gordon Isaacs (coordinator of SWEAT) had spoken some introductory comments, I nervously stepped on the platform that served as a stage. Encouraging my voice to be loud but casual, I mentioned my research intentions and that I would bring snacks and offer travel money each time an informal interview was set up, but that I was only looking into the experiences of foreign men. During the five-minute 'smoke break' that followed, I was approached by four men who offered to work with me. However, the challenges in arranging frequent meetings continued. It was not disinterest that presented itself as a challenge as I had suspected after the first meeting. There were multiple factors that made it difficult for the men to keep their appointments. A major factor was weather conditions. Usually on foot but also on minibus taxis and trains, some of the men have to cover long distances and make an effort to come to SWEAT, where the first interviews were arranged, during which other meeting spots could be discussed.

Rainy days at the beginning of the research period made it difficult for participants to keep their appointments, which they would not cancel because most of them do not own a cell phone and public phones are costly, often vandalized and not always within reach. Another very important factor that ties in with the argument of this thesis is that, for precariously living male refugees in Cape Town, the hierarchy of priorities is adjustable, depending on the kinds of opportunities that present themselves. For instance, an arrangement to meet me and receive travel money could be quite lucrative, but if a construction or gardening job became available the same day offering more income, our meeting would be of a lower priority. In two cases, longer-term work arrangements came up and prevented informants from being available on a regular basis.

In my efforts to arrange interviews, multiple issues, dominating debates in contemporary anthropology, came to the fore. One of them is the challenged notion that fieldwork ought to be of 'longue durée' (Braudel, 1958) in order to transcend a situational analysis. Participant observation is as central to anthropology as the concept of 'the field' and is just as historically constructed. It is meant to involve long-term contact and proximity to a group of people or 'culture' (Bernard, 1998). To gain an 'emic' perspective (that is to understand the world from 'the native's point of view', as Geertz (1973) has suggested), time is essential in establishing intimate relationships. By implication, this would mean that shorter periods, often limited by forces out of the researcher's control, render it impossible to create an ethnographic account of academic value. While I agree that a period of time long enough to conduct research in a relaxed atmosphere is of great importance in establishing a good rapport with informants (which is why I decided to continue meeting my informants for longer than the designated time-frame by the university), whether or not there is an atmosphere of intimacy is something that is not just dependant of factors of time and cannot be one-sidedly manufactured. The willingness of potential participants to open up depends on the kinds of relationships that become possible in a particular space with a particular person and this depends on a variety of factors, such as gatekeepers, compatibilities, communication and, plainly, feelings of likability. Whether or not a relationship and good rapport become possible also depends on whether the researcher is able to step out of this role and is willing to make themselves vulnerable.

The historical subject–object distinction in anthropology (Collins & Gallinat, 2013) and authoritative ideas of doing research 'on' someone (Clifford, 1988) became blurred in the sharing of some of my own stories when asked about my personal life and when empathizing with my informants when they shared theirs. Spending time in spaces that are part of the participants' day-to-day lives made this somewhat easier for me to establish connections and I soon came to perceive the men as more than just my informants.

As I can neither participate in peoples' dreams nor observe them in a 'traditional' ethnographic sense, my dependency on narrations as a source of information is where anthropology and its research methodologies could be argued to constitute insufficient tools to create an informative account. However, Hollan states that 'the kind of dreams people report can be related to the problems they confront at particular stages of life and to the inter-subjective context of the interview itself' (2004:171). I am certain that subconscious and imaginative processes do not only translate onto 'real-life' experiences but that they themselves are shaped by the issues the men are confronted with. What is more, they are relived in some form in the process of narrating them as a story. Ethnography as 'thick description' (Geertz, 1973) offers the most intimate lens through which individual experiences can be recorded as a basis for interpretation, even if such interpretations merely offer 'partial truths' (Clifford, 1986), composed through the researcher's memories and experiences.

Another question that presented itself during my fieldwork was that of appropriate means and modes of exchange for information. Offering money to informants as a compensation for their help and time tends to be seen as a direct exchange of money for information in the social sciences – and not just for any information but the kind the informant believes the researcher to be looking for. Money might thus interfere with the dynamics between researcher and informant. However, Bernard has argued that interviewees 'should be paid at least the local rate for their time' (Bernard, 2013:182). It took some time to find informants that I would be able to see more than once and three of them encouraged meetings after the period of data collection. In learning just how precarious the living conditions were for the men I encountered, I found the arrangement of offering R40 'travel money' per meeting (as SWEAT offers) to be a fair one, even if the amount could be subject of discussion. It had to be taken into consideration that meeting me for an interview for one–two hours meant that, within this time and the time spent travelling to meet up with me, my informants would be deprived of the opportunity to organise work or food to sustain themselves for the day (or perhaps the next few days).

I came to acknowledge our meetings as a gift of insights and put some thought into finding ways of reciprocating (apart from the travel money) and put attention into packing picnics and lending my ear. Furthermore, I threw a little 'thank you' party at the end of my official stay at SWEAT, prepared food and brought soft drinks. I also grew some seedlings at home, which I then planted in the still winter-scarce food garden of the organisation with some of the men enthusiastically offering their help. I was also invited to the men's' graduation at the end of the 14-week period of their support group (equalling seven meetings) where they were provided with certificates of completion. Given how my relationship with the men unfolded, I am fairly certain that my offering of travel money was not understood as a standardisation of interchangeable experience.

Having internalised the participant observation paradigm so dominant in anthropology, I was keen to follow my informants around and to see how they live and what their days look like. However, as there hardly ever was a fixed plan for the day and my informants were reluctant to take me to their township homes or to their sleeping places in town, this was not possible to the degree I had hoped for. Reasons brought to me were security-related (applying to myself and them) and based on the insistence that these places were not for 'a lady' to see. I tried to convey that I am rather thick-skinned and that there was no need to be concerned about my judgment of their living situation. I realised that thinking of ethnography as 'the more intimate the more holistic and better', I almost disregarded boundaries of privacy. What is more, occupied with my self-portrayal as tough and open-minded, I nearly missed rather important statements that were made about the different spaces in which the men spend time, making it clear that they had ambiguous feelings about their 'homes' and the spaces in which they spend their 'leisure time' - which are sometimes simultaneously the spaces in which they encounter their clients. Matthew, for instance, made it very clear that I was not welcome to see his sleeping spot, which, he says, is rough but has become home.

The men who stay in townships spend most days in town and usually take the last train back before it gets dark. Understanding everyday choices and dreams, required an understanding of the men's experiences across time and space and thus a form of multi-sited ethnography (Marcus, 1995). Due to a lack of access to some of the locations in which they spend their time, I had to try and trace the links between the different locations and the meanings attached to them in an imaginative fashion and without always being able to experience them through my own body.

Since I had summarised my research to be about 'foreign, male sex workers', some of the men talked freely about sex with clients but others hesitated or offered very brief responses to questions that focused on sex work. At a later stage of the research, I became aware that some of the men do sex work rather infrequently, usually if there are no other sources of income available at the time or if they encounter someone offering to reciprocate financially for some form of sexual encounter or company by fluke. Attraction and being able to form some kind of connection with the person would also play a role. However, frequency of transactional sex does not necessarily imply that the men identified themselves as 'sex workers'. When I mentioned SWEAT during the interviews, the men notably embodied being sex workers and talked about 'sex work' and 'doing' business, often using human rights language. However, it became apparent that this identity was only highlighted when it seemed contextually appropriate. Hence, the focus of my research shifted from 'foreign, male sex workers' to 'male refugee bodies' and how they are employed to survive and to dream with.

I spent most of my time in the field sitting outside with my informants, watching the movements around us and engaging in conversations that I moderated as little as possible. As we were getting to know one another and I was asking informants questions about 'back home' and about Cape Town, I was also urged to share stories about Germany and my hometown, Offenbach. I was asked about my studies and what kind of job I wanted to do in the future. Due to the ambiguity of the different spaces the men occupied and the intimate conversations we were having in spaces where there was constant movement around us, boundaries between 'public' and 'private' became blurred. Through the sometimes vividly told stories shared with me, I felt as though I was taking part in my informants' experiences on some level, even if there was no particular everyday routine I could physically follow and in spite of some stories taking place in the past or in the men's imagination. Descriptions of stories that happened long ago were sometimes more capturing and detailed than descriptions of the recent past and it became apparent that verbalising them made them part of the men's present experience in that they could cause pain or pleasure in the very moment of being told. Likewise, descriptions of possible future scenarios could be very vivid and seemed almost graspable. Thus, it was not only the line supposedly dividing the 'private' and 'public' that became obscured but also temporal divides of the present, past and future.

In anthropology, heavy emphasis lies on the 'now' and the aspect of 'being there' and witnessing things as they happen. In limiting experiences to a particular time and geographic place (which is part of the fetishisation of 'the field' that Gupta and Ferguson [1997] have challenged) the researcher may potentially fail to see space-making as a process that is strongly influenced by past experiences and ideas of the future. Gupta and Ferguson (1997) have argued that ideas of culture, identity and space ought to be seen as fluid and anthropologists can no longer represent 'a culture' of 'a people' as belonging to a certain place, especially since people become increasingly mobile. I am of the opinion that binding cultural experience to a particular moment in time is just as problematic and I am going to employ life histories as a means of bringing the past and anticipated future into the present ethnographic moment. I was allowed to experience life histories through the moments their sharing created, helping me to grapple with the ways in which the men's social positions and identities are constantly reworked and negotiated, sometimes by transcending time and space.

Marcus (1995) argues that life histories as a multi-sited research approach reveal juxtapositions of social contexts through a succession of narrated individual experiences. He also states that they are potential guides to the delineation of ethnographic spaces within systems that are shaped by categorical distinctions, which may render these spaces otherwise invisible. Life histories thus reveal unexpected associations between sites and social contexts. While it may be tempting to reduce the lives of foreign, male sex workers in Cape Town to 'invisibilised' sites of struggle, I decided to look at them as de-linear ethnographic spaces, accommodating multiple relationships and potentialities for the men to make themselves visible on their own terms. In this regard, life histories helped me gain a better understanding of how people, spaces and dreams relate. Taking into consideration that there are shifts between various life worlds as well as between scenarios of differently negotiated expectations the men are confronted with – at home and at work, from the distance, within intimate encounters as well as by strangers – it is important not to isolate the moment from the narrative altogether. The resonance of the individual self and how it relates to the body, objects and people (Hollan, 2004) is embedded in a bigger story, without which a collection of single dream stories would become detached from the individual.

In terms of recording devices and privacy, I did not anticipate any problems as the voice recorder I was using was meant to serve my memory and not for anyone else's ears, which I pointed out to my informants. They were all quick to agree that I could use it after this explanation. I asked for permission every time I started a recording of an interview and was soon dismissed for this. Sam, perhaps half-jokingly said that I did not have to keep asking and that, after all, he did not have that 'thing that other people call privacy'. I replied that he should still think about what he would like to keep 'private' and he responded with one of his friendly laughs. Other informants sometimes asked, after having spoken for a while, whether the recorder was still running and Scott asked me after our second meeting what the apparatus did. There was obviously some concern that I had not picked up before. When I explained that it was recording voice Scott replied 'ah, only voice'.

These instances made it clear to me that my informants were sometimes more and sometimes less conscious of their stories being captured. I explained that going through the interviews again on audio would be useful for me in selecting themes for my written work and my participants seemed more relaxed after I had offered information about how I intend to process the 'data' I was collecting. It seemed to me as though the recorder was less taken note of thereafter and was forgotten about soon after having been placed between me and the informant. Nevertheless, the comments above made me wonder about the extent to which being introduced as a researcher via SWEAT is associated with a right to intrude into lives and to demand information as detailed and personal as possible. I started to deliberately draw attention to the recorder at the beginning of conversations to remind my informants that they could decide what to share in the hope of creating an opportunity to redefine the 'private' with the beginning of each meeting.

My own body played a relevant role in doing research as it was often seen as a form of social capital, perhaps sometimes a dangerous one. When sitting in the park in Woodstock with Sam or Matthew, one of the local men would usually come over to greet me but he would not greet my company and neither would they greet him. Instead, my interview partners would turn their heads so that their faces were less visible. Scott, 35-years old from Tanzania, told me that this particular person was a gang member. Even though Scott tended to make sweeping statements about locals, this made me think about the conflicts my presence could potentially cause. I was also told that some of the men coming to the space were robbed of their travel money by other attendees right after the meeting. I became aware of the tensions and sub-groups within the 'Creative Space' and realised that the men I knew from the support group (made up of foreigners only) never seemed to contribute in the discussion groups when there were locals present.

I did attract a lot of attention in the 'Creative Space' meetings. There would always be a number of men who approached me and engaged me in a conversation. Sometimes they would argue over who would sit next to me. I started responding to this using humour and learned which groups to stick to in order to avoid flirtatious approaches. This made me envisage my body as carrying symbolic meaning in itself in this particular space and as something many of the men liked to be associated with. I generally preferred to sit with the foreign men I knew as my informants on a big step, dangling our feet in the air above an old train line, overgrown with grass and leading nowhere. The rest of the men would be scattered in the yard or waiting inside the hall for the meeting to start. One day, when a group of local men who told me that they wanted to start a choir presented their skills to me, I realised that making it a routine to sit with my informants in this social space might put them in a difficult position.

My presence could thus cause different kinds of reactions, which were not necessarily limited to my own experiences. One of them, especially in this space but also in others, could be pride associated with being seen with me. At the same time, attracting attention is what my research participants were generally trying to avoid. At the very least it can be said that there is care and concern involved in the ways in which the men allow for themselves to be visible – depending on the particular context (I will return to this point later on). My body became a symbol for certain privileges to which the men do not have access and which are associated with my being commonly identified as white, female and seemingly economically well off. In the tie of the 'crisis of representation' in anthropology and efforts to avoid radical alterity, descriptions of people and social phenomena should be particularly reflective and context-specific, and should convey a clear idea of as many particularities of the spaces inhabited (as well as their politics) as possible. This is precisely what I hope to have put into practice in my account on male refugees in Cape Town.

Chapter 5

Bodies taking shape:
On corporeal resistance to societal exclusion

This chapter is concerned with the shape everyday life takes for foreign men seeking refuge in Cape Town and the ways in which this shape becomes modified from different angles. I will furthermore discuss how social practice in this context is tied to notions of time and the perceptual self by referring to Csordas's (1994) reflections on corporeal experience. The physical plays an essential role as the men find themselves in a constant state of emergency, especially during winter in Cape Town, when opportunities to make money nearly cease. Most of the men at SWEAT make do with what is at hand (a framework introduced by Lévi-Strauss (1966) as bricolage) by applying combinations of the limited resources available to new problems and opportunities. This chapter focuses on the immediate need to maintain the body as quintessential stabilising tool. I am arguing that, in maintaining and making use of the body every day, strategies come to the fore through which people reclaim humanness and forms of citizenship in precarious contexts in which they are conceptualised as lesser (see Allison, 2012; Butler, 2016; Biehl, 2007; Standing, 2011; Stewart, 2012) or 'ex-human' (Biehl, 2007).

The very physical and concrete experiences of the everyday have to be placed in a larger neoliberal system in which male refugee bodies are prone to be rendered exploitable and disposable (Standing, 2011). The constant challenging of the men's bodily integrity (by being exploited as workers, forced to eat from bins, being kept in jail over the weekend, etc.) does not simply become embodied and reproduced. Instead, the men find niches in society which allow them to reconceptualise their experiential selves. These niches, social spheres invisible to most, allow for the continuation of dreams. Making use of these, social boundaries, designed to keep refugees in places designated to the poor in Cape Town, can be transcended - imaginatively and strategically. Physical strategies employed in maintaining, nourishing and sheltering the body can be interpreted as forms of resisting domination (De Certeau, 1984) and so can the men's dreams. I am thus going to conceptualise the men's bodies as 'forums of expressions' (Lock, 1993) in which memories of the past and daily corporeal experiences become interpreted and negotiated.

Discourses in contemporary Cape Town become inscribed onto the bodies of male refugees, which in turn become symbols and constant reminders, to themselves and others, of societal values and differentiations. This embodied symbolism is a unique reflection of a broader theme, one of neo-liberalism and state capitalism, violating the right of equal pay for equal work as well as the right to free movement (Sichone, 2008). Bodily inscriptions also reflect global tendencies to capitalise on a disposable mass of bodies, discouraged from forms of societal participation that would offer them a voice (Standing, 2011). Having voice and being recognised as equal serve as mantras in the organisation SWEAT when framing possibilities within a tight legal and social framework, but also with regards to the prospect of a future scenario in which sex work is legalised and de-stigmatised. In a more pressing sense, SWEAT offers support in maintaining oneself as a sex worker. Once a week, food can be accessed as well as the R40 'travel money'. The support system with regards to health and legal issues SWEAT offers to those who are often denied help by public institutions also forms part of this immediate support. Not less importantly, SWEAT intends to offer a safe space to socialise, establish contacts and exchange knowledge and tips. For refugees, establishing themselves in Cape Town firstly means maintaining their own bodies, even if that is through bodily sacrifice of various degrees, which may take the form of the risk of unprotected sex, the risk of working and living in crime-ridden environments or doing risky labour on building sites for sometimes less than R50 per day. The forms of labour exploitation the men are exposed to require creativity and flexibility in the process of being dealt with and shape narratives in different ways. I will offer two partial life stories that were shared with me in order to highlight the ways in which the men's journeys impact their experienced notions of self and the spaces that become available in the process of negotiating life in foreign Cape Town.

The body as a hindrance

35-year-old Scott from Tanzania had been in Cape Town for two years. Before that, he explained, he was deported from South Africa a few times and forced to return to Tanzania – only to start his journey again: 'I was only 21 years old that [first] time. We were jumping the fence at the border. Not like you guys who come with a passport on a plane and stuff.' His bigger goal was to hide in one of the ships departing for Europe, America or Canada, which is why he took a job as a cleaner at the harbour. This shows a political subjectivity of bodies that can easily be moved across different spaces. Scott had never been in a long-term partnership and did not have pressing responsibilities in Tanzania. His mother had her own source of income, selling samosas[9] and renting out rooms. He would like to send her some money every now and then, he explained, but could not remember the last time he had managed to do so. Scott would take the train from Delft, an informal settlement) every morning (unless it was a Sunday or the weather conditions did not accommodate it) and would get off at the train station in the city centre, from where he would proceed to the Grand Parade in search of clients. If his search was futile here, he would often make his way to the library to use the internet or to read. He would then walk to a park in the city centre, again in search of clients but also to meet friends. This is where he would spend most of his day before taking the last train back to Delft, just before it gets dark.

In Delft, he stayed with a friend, whom he had met when looking for a safe sleeping spot around town. When his friend (a South African citizen) got offered temporary housing by the city of Cape Town, he invited Scott to join him. Scott told me about his girlfriend at the park and explained shyly that she would be biologically identified as male. From her, he was offered friendship, company and sexual contact. He described her touch quite vividly to me and smiled when talking about her. However, he did not approve of her having transactional sex with others and being involved with gang members, with whom she also shared sexual experiences as well as drugs. His girlfriend had disclosed her HIV-positive status to him and Scott claimed to have his 'own ways' of preventing contracting the virus.

While sex work was not Scott's only source of income and was, in fact, described by him as an unreliable one, he spent

---

[9] Fried pastries, usually with savory filling, which are also commonly sold in small shops across South Africa.

most of his time sitting in the park, shifting his physical position only slightly every now and then. It is through contacts that he was sometimes offered a job in construction work or other manual labour. He took these opportunities when they arose and sometimes joined the crowds of people offering cheap labour on many roadsides of Cape Town. For sex, he was seldom offered much. Only the tourists in summer, adding to the more sporadic movements in the park during winter, offered what he considers 'good money' for a sexual encounter with him. Locals, he said, mostly ask him to 'do it for fun' with them in a public bathroom or in a building, central to the city, which offers big, shared rooms for sex for a R30 entrance fee per person. He sometimes went home having spent more money on train tickets than he had made and often goes without a paying client for days or even weeks. Scott expressed concern about the future and getting older. He worried that his body could not be relied on as a source of income in the years to come.

One of his very vividly told stories is rather exemplifying for the kinds of pressures that he was confronted with on an everyday basis. He described how a client had recently offered him R200 to penetrate him in a public bathroom and how he could not get an erection to complete the job. It was with squeakiness in his voice that he illustrated these two R100 bills and how his body had prevented him from accessing this cushioning financial buffer. Towards the end of our first meeting in the park, Scott and I walked towards the train station together. Along the way, I remembered the sandwich I had made for him and forgotten to give him earlier. When I handed it to him, his expression changed from broadly smiling, the way I knew it up until then, to frozen. In an alarmed tone he asked me whether this meant that I was not going to give him the R40 travel money. I was reminded of how precarity hits the very core of the men's existence, which is maintained through food and other essentials to surviving but also by ensuring access to social spaces that are associated with opportunities for jobs and companionship. This particular experience also made me more conscious of the selectiveness with which the men shared their stories and the various nuances these bear.

Scott's story illustrates some of the challenges shared by many of the male refugees I encountered, who would take on all kinds of physical labour in order to maintain themselves and increase their mobility and corporeal value at least temporarily. Scott's body seemed to be simultaneously carrier of hope and pain. It can also be seen as a barrier to aspirations as, in his mind, he had left the African continent a long time ago. When talking about the future, it sounded as though it was just a matter of time until he would arrive somewhere in Europe. His story shows how establishing oneself in Cape Town as a foreign, African man with little resources is a process during which social relations are of great significance in finding access to work, sleeping spaces and supportive relationships. In spite of this form of social dependency, Scott, as did many of the other men, emphasised the importance of not relying on anybody 'back home', financially or otherwise. Along with the experience of financial independence, freedom in shaping their own lives was emphasised as the upside of lacking closely- knit kinship networks to fall back upon. At the same time, all the men expressed the wish to have a partnership or family on their own at some point, but indicated that they had to improve their lives before this would be possible. Their bodies can thus be seen as longing for relationships, substantiating stability. The oldest two of my informants, Scott and Issa (35 and 38 years old), saw there to be a time limit attached to their current survival strategies and were both thinking about the need to develop a retirement plan that does not involve sex work in the near future.

As Butler (2016) has put it, interdependency constitutes us as social and embodied, as vulnerable and passionate with our thinking getting us nowhere without the presuppositions of the sustaining conditions of life. The ways in which the men were using their bodies to survive and stabilise their lives were often seen as a temporary strategy in the face of precarity and a lack of reliable and sustaining structures, but seemed sometimes more or less permanent and sometimes occasional, sustained by individual, their specific assets, encounters, the reliability of their networks and dependant on how pressing perceived needs for an alternatively imagined future pronounced itself.

The body told

Sam, 29-years old, is from Zimbabwe and had been in Cape Town for two years. His physical presence stood out. Sam walked tall, sticking out his wide chest, but not in a provocative way. There was something humble in his confident presence that confused me. In some moments he seemed almost shy during our conversations and would not look at me for a long time. His skin looked healthy and radiant and he seemed to have numerous items of clothing, even if they were slightly damaged. He outlined his story as a series of happenings, leading to radical changes in a life that had already been framed by sudden and unexpected shifts, resulting in physical and psychological insecurities. At this point in time, he said, he was doing any temporary jobs he could find - 'too keep me going', as he put it. He found most of his infrequent male and female clients on an online platform for people looking for- and offering sexual pleasure. The stories he told me made me feel as though they were not just directed towards me, but re-designed for me in particular, and that telling them enabled Sam to come to terms with his past and present decisions by manifesting himself through my memory in a specific way.

Sam's mother died when he was 11 years old. His father remarried and died when Sam was 16. His stepmother decided to move away and spent the money his father had left behind for schooling on other things. Sam managed to get money when the house he had grown up in was sold and used it to pay his remaining school fees, as well as the school fees for his at the time 12- year-old brother Matthew, whom he was taking care of and whom I knew from SWEAT as well. When the economy started getting worse in Zimbabwe and he could not make enough money from renting out the rooms of another family property in order to cover electricity and water bills, he started a second-hand phone and fridge repair shop. One day, the area in which he lived and worked was cleared by the government and all the shops and houses were bulldozed. He saw no choice but to leave his products by the roadside, because he had nowhere to take them. Sam decided to leave Matthew with his aunt for the time he was still attending school and made his way to Botswana in search for work. When this proved to be futile, he moved to Johannesburg, and stayed in Hillbrow, an area known to be particularly violent (see Mpe, 2001) and had a stable job as a rubble-truck driver for a couple of years there. However, he describes life in the area as extremely risky and paints a picture of sheer brutality. Sam went back to see Matthew in Zimbabwe and returned to South Africa on an expiring work permit, which added the likelihood of being deported (Johannesburg officials are known amongst the men to follow deportation regulations more strictly than officials in Cape Town) to the insecurities that came with being without a job, a safe place to stay or a reliable social network in place.

Having a contact there, he moved to Cape Town in search of greener pastures and was introduced to the city and shown places where he could try to find work. Sam started working at a restaurant at the V&A Waterfront and shared a flat in Mowbray (one of the more affluent suburbs of the city) for a while, until he had enough money saved up to buy a car. He then started working as a taxi driver and managed to establish a regular local clientele to get him through the winter, during which a lack of tourism drags down the taxi business in the city.

When Sam had to go back to Zimbabwe for a funeral and to 'organise some things', he sold his car and gave his belongings to friends for storage, but never heard from most of them again. When he returned from Zimbabwe via Johannesburg to Cape Town, all his papers, including his passport and driver's license, were stolen at the hostel at which he was staying, radically stripping him of lucrative work opportunities and forcing him into adopting the status of a 'refugee'.

Upon his return to Cape Town, he found that none of his 'friends' were willing to support him and ended up moving to the informal settlement Philippi. Since winter was approaching, he could not get his old job as a waiter back due to staff cuts at this time of the year. He explained that the lack of other work opportunities led him to start engaging in sex work. From a friend, he learnt that he could use websites in order to offer company, which may or may not lead to sexual contact. Searching for clients online also has the benefit that he could see a picture of them first and decide if he 'could do it', as he put it. Sam also spent a lot of his time in the city centre, visiting Matthew (who is living there by himself and without stable shelter) and friends or using the internet at the library in town to organise work.

Some parts of Sam's story sounded slightly rehearsed, perhaps a survival strategy in dealing with authorities and potential financial supporters. He detailed his various returns to Zimbabwe and his relationships while looking into the distance, as if absorbed in thought. Sam seemed to take pride in managing to stay in one of the most dangerous townships, and highlighted the risks of his living situation. He also pointed out his sense of responsibility when describing how he was taking care of finances at home and Matthew after his parents had died.

Sam and his stories offer a good example for the flexible and strategic use of the body, a necessity for many refugees in Cape Town, especially during winter - but also of the stories that become embodied as part of manoeuvring the city. Sam presented himself as a free man who makes his own choices, even when he would find himself in particularly challenging situations. He was the one who agentively determined the direction of his life and rendered a future possible in spite of numerous existential obstacles, for instance in avoiding sex with men whenever possible in order to maintain himself as a 'marriable' man, as he explained. Sam also said he avoided 'sugar mommies' as they would make him feel like a 'slave' and thus undermine his sense of self. He therefore negotiated his income-generating practices constantly and reflectively with his long-term well-being in mind.

There appears to be a lot of thought and mindfulness involved in the telling of Sam's life story, re-constructible or not, and I could sense that the descriptions in this specific version of himself as told to me was meant to appeal to both, me and him. The confidence and sense of self that 'telling himself' produced can be seen as another strategy of living precariously or, in a sense, even for survival (also see Malaquais, 2001; Ndjio, 2006; Ndjio, 2008 on 'confidence men').

Strategic aspects in manoeuvring the city

In the following section, I elaborate on specific strategies that became relevant in narratives of surviving, being and becoming as a refugee in Cape Town.

Being available
The establishing of direct networks with customers and other potential employers was rendered difficult for the men with whom I worked, as most of them did not own a cell phone. This meant that they could not be hired on short notice, except for Daniel - the only one of the men who had a room in the suburbs, in University Estate. Daniel was offered this room by an older woman, a relative of one of his employees. He was charged rent only when he had money 'coming in' and explained that his hostess knew that he would pay when he was able to. By presenting himself as reliable to an employer, establishing networks and obtaining shelter in a comparably secure space, Daniel managed to avoid some of the riskiness of the everyday of being a refugee in Cape Town. Around his home, he could move more freely, accumulate things that make everyday life easier and require less planning. Living inside a house in a more affluent suburb, he was more likely to manage holding onto things, which the other men struggled with.

Daniel took a short-term work opportunity to show himself in a certain light and thereby challenged the notion of a disposable (Standing, 2011) body, shaped, moulded and undermined by a particular form of labour exploitation. The physical locations the men inhabited and the politics within these are closely tied to the ways in which the men could manoeuvre within them (see Salo, 2010; 2013 on townships) and the material realities of their everyday lives.

Recycling consumerism

Foods and objects that other people dispose of in garbage bins and elsewhere constitute an important source to maintain the existence of the superficially less resourceful. The very act of having to collect these things is symbolic for the rigorous divisions in terms of the attribution of value to humans in Cape Town, and constituted one of the strategies the men employed in sustaining their bodies. The divide between first-hand consumers on the one end, and recycling-consumers on the other end of the social scale in Cape Town serves as a reminder of what constitutes 'fully human' in this context. The value of things disposed of by some becomes revitalised for it to be now used by others. While one part of society is able to purchase and partially or temporarily consume enough to sustain others with the 'garbage' they produce in the process, the 'left-overs' of excessive consumption become crucial for the latter. The act of physically collecting from bins in public spaces forces people to perform the societal role they are urged into and leads to other people being able to observe, recognise and re-enforce this positionality. What Sharp (2000) calls the 'integrity' of the body becomes undermined and second-hand consumers are forced even further into 'zones of social abandonment' (Biehl, 2007). Through an exclusion from many spaces associated with being social, the men were constantly reminded that there was no permanent space in this context for them to occupy. Back in Tanzania, Scott used to enjoy going to the movies, but did not feel welcome to do so in Cape Town and would thus not end up going, even if he had a movie ticket. The sticking to very particular social zones is due to the insecurities facilitated by being objectified as a refugee, as non-belonging and thus a lesser human.

Finding and living a niche existence

Being a refugee in an informal settlement, referred to as 'location' by the men, presents a challenge that calls for distinct strategies. For Sam and Issa, inhabiting and manoeuvring these spaces safely required making themselves visible and known to some degree in order to establish relationships with their South African neighbours. Alcohol served as a means for this, either in being bought and shared at somebody's home or at a shebeen (a local bar). Issa spoke of the necessity to spend money on his neighbours in this way to prevent people in the settlement to '... come and take that money by force'. His observations of the local conduct taught him that he had to '[...] pretend to be friends. I know they need to drink with friends', he explained. Alcohol thus served as both, social lubricant and as prop in a survival strategy. Being surrounded by South Africans may help, but not necessarily because they would be willing to defend a foreign man in an attack. Rather, surrounding oneself with local tongues served to drown foreign accents and thus as camouflaging safety coat. As Issa put it: 'If they see you as a foreigner – where is he going to go? Which police is going to listen to him?'. However, such strategies, intended to contain precarity, are not without their very own sets of challenges. Contacts with locals were seen as ambiguous and managing them became balance act in efforts to avoid becoming 'too visible' and known in informal settlements.

Being shelterless in town requires its own know-how. Sleeping in groups was considered to be safer than sleeping alone and sleeping spots cannot be too remote. As Scott phrased it: 'If you sleep somewhere alone and something happens – it's your fault. Don't hide yourself; you can scream and scream'. In line with this thinking, some of the men slept in larger groups on sports fields or would find other shadows of town life within which to settle for the night or throughout the day. 25-year-old Miguel from Mozambique made friends with two older men and stayed with them further up the mountain, but not too far from the city centre. This social constellation, like any other friendship, was built on mutual trust but also relied on concrete support. With Miguel's description of his evenings in this protective circle, a movie scene composed itself in my mind: a young man sitting by the fire, musing, smoking a joint and looking down upon the city centre, glistening with lights in the darkness. Matthew, on the other hand, slept alone, resisting such 'rules' of street life. He claimed that he is not a 'social' person and refused to stay with his brother Sam in a township shack (an improvised and likely impermanent structure), arguing that he is 'better off this way'. Through his explanations and descriptions of his daily life, Matthew rationalised his decision, and described the precariousness of loneliness and almost complete isolation as a rite of passage to manhood, ultimately making him stronger. The only one disrupting this lonely mission to manhood was Sam, who would come to check on him, bring him food and arrange jobs for him here and there.

Applying skills and knowledge in selling sex and company

Using the body by offering sex in exchange for money can take different forms. Escort work requires being organised and having access to the Internet, as well as a phone (urgent offers may expire by the time emails are checked and replied to in an internet café). It also requires different skills than other forms of sex work. Being an actor, listening to the client and raising his or her self-esteem are part of the required skill-set. Another skill is knowing how much personal information to reveal. When being approached by potential clients on the street or in parks, it is not stage talents that are of significance but negotiating skills and being able to protect oneself from ending up in situations one is not ready to involve one's body and mind in.

The men offered sex and company in more or less organised ways and frequencies. There were also different associations attached to sex work, depending on the clientele and practices. Daniel, for instance, spent his days in Sea Point, hoping to meet clients while, at the same time, using his contacts in the area to organise food and cigarette money. He considered sex work to be a better alternative to stealing, something he used to do. As long as he is not the one to be penetrated, he quickly added. Daniel often has no clients for weeks, and some contacts, he claimed, only desire spending time with him, drinking wine and watching TV. He thus did not consider himself to be a 'real' sex worker. When Daniel came to Cape Town from Mozambique via Johannesburg seven years prior me meeting him, he had to learn how to go about finding clients, as did the other men. 'For me it was a friend of mine who told me. Because I was doing it, but the wrong way. You see. So a friend of mine said no, you have to go this way. So that's how I come to know'. Daniel distinguished 'dating', a practice involving money, which he had been doing in Mozambique, and 'business' (a synonym for sex work) in Cape Town. He insisted that when he was out of a job and thus 'doing business', it was only with women; even though my other conversations had revealed that male clients are the norm. For Sam, sex work is 'just something I can use to get out of this situation' and for Scott it constituted a practice that may, at some point, help him change his life drastically (I will return to this in the next chapter).

The strategies acquired while manoeuvring Cape Town, knowing which networks to nourish, where and how to sleep, eat, and earn an income – however infrequent, risky and badly paid – are continuous processes and require the employment of different skills and strategies, which often have to be carefully navigated and flexibly adjusted. It is these processes and the demands of life in Cape Town (in terms of needing to be observant, adjustable and keeping a low- profile) that shape the men's multiple notions of self in different encounters. I am arguing that the objectification of the male refugee body and the requirements attached to this existence in the study context is not simply being reproduced, but that the body-self is defined and re-defined in a continuous process of becoming oriented in the city and in exposure to various challenges.

I would like to stress that 'being foreign' is not the single deciding factor influencing the lives of people seeking refuge of some kind in Cape Town. Other factors and happenstances may determine the path of a particular life story. Shawn, for instance, had a fancy apartment in the southern suburbs and earned up to R3000 by spending one weekend with foreign businessmen. I was given his contact details through a person who works at SWEAT and met him at his apartment in Kenilworth. Shawn is from Uganda and acquired his degree in

Business Administration there. Just after finishing his exams, he set off to Cape Town, having met a local farm owner in an online forum and having been invited to live with him. However, the relationship turned sour and Shawn was thrown out of his lover's house one day without his papers, which the latter refused to return to him. Via a friend of his former lover, he learnt that he could get paid for sex, without even having to negotiate, by submitting himself to the friend's needs on a regular basis. Through another man he met, Shawn put up an online profile as an escort. However, one of his regular clients, who moved between Holland and South Africa, organised a job for him at his company doing desktop work as he wanted them to have a sexually exclusive relationship. Shawn found the money from the office job to be insufficient and refused to give up his regular clients, but agreed to disable his web-profile as an escort. Shawn's story could have ended differently, with a number of factors playing a role, such as having a university degree, access to the Internet and thus particular kinds of encounters, which helped him move within a particular social sphere in Cape Town. While Shawn may not struggle to physically maintain himself, his rather comfortable existence is dependent on maintaining his lover's interest in him and is therefore still precarious.

Scott (1990) argues that the dominant in a society never control the stage absolutely, but that their wishes normally prevail. Those wishes typically generate insults and slights to human dignity, which, in turn, foster a 'hidden transcript of indignation' (Scott, 1990). In order to identify different forms of domination, he suggests, one has to look at the kinds of indignities the exercise of power routinely produces and the hidden transcripts – used by the oppressed as a form of resistance – instead of merely focusing on the public protocol.

According to the public protocol, male refugees are denied a life of comfort, visibility and feeling of self-worth. In establishing relationships and skilfully developing strategies that enabled the men to stay relatively safe in certain niches of Cape Town, they managed to produce a transcript that is largely hidden to a dehumanising gaze.

The surviving body also comprises of the ageing body, the body in relationships, the body as a barrier, the body changing and longing and the body in other corporeal states of transformation. Bodies never simply are - but they are in a continuous state of becoming. Male refugees in Cape Town occupy different body-selves in different contexts and shift between spaces in which they largely become objectified as worthless (as they are rendered foreign and made vulnerable to local structures at the same time) and thus create spaces for themselves in which they can transcend this objectification. Within these processes, it is not just the body that is involved, but also the mind. While, juristically, the refugee body is seen as easy to categorise, move and to manage, Mbembe's (1992) reflections on embodiment highlight that the body becomes playground of both, oppression and resistance.

This is where hegemonic and counter-hegemonic practices, authority and subversion, power and defiance meet. Male refugees in Cape Town become moulded into powerless denizens (Standing, 2011) and are seen as a static category, captured in a time–space vacuum. However, I am arguing that their multiple, fragmented body-selves and their experiences and understandings of time, space, self, body and identity play their counter-active part in a process of strategically negotiating being objectified and exploited.

This chapter attempted to grapple with the ways in which being forced into a state of urgency and emergency impacts on the strategies male refugees employ in managing their bodies as survival and stabilising tools. The following chapter aims to reveal more about bodies in a process of becoming and about how male refugees dream and reconstruct themselves imaginatively.

Chapter 6

Dream until your dreams come true? On bodily mappings of self

This chapter illustrates that dreams may serve as a way of reclaiming and nurturing the very humanness male refugees are stripped of on a daily basis, as highlighted in the previous chapter. Dreams thus offer an additional bodily strategy of navigating the city and bringing about certainty in the face of multiple uncertainties by re-imagining and legitimising one's presence in spaces from which one seems to be excluded. I will start off with a critical discussion of dreaming as a useful concept in examining and understanding the men's predicaments. This will be followed by an engagement with the different dreams male refugees in Cape Town have and with the modes by which these dreams are sought to be achieved in the face of precarity.

The state of precarity, imbued with being a 'non-citizen' or 'denizen' (Standing, 2011), incorporates being excluded from many forms of social support, the likelihood of being forced into exploitative labour and the need to be visible to the 'right' degree without attracting too much attention to one's physical existence. It also means being exposed to others in that the men have to knit relationships and, to some degree, depend on people who may or may not understand their situation while looking for independence in Cape Town. They are thus not only living a life shaped by precarity, but also a life modified through precariousness (Butler, 2016), due to a lack of broader support. In the following section, I am going to discuss dreams as alternative platforms for visibility for refugees, incorporating memories and the capacity to imagine the future. Dreams can be seen as a way of achieving a sense of belonging, as they offer a form of engaging with the discrepancy of a constantly undermined body-self and the various meanings that become inscribed onto the men's bodies via different spaces and their politics. In their corporeality, they thus help bridging troubled and precarious waters. I am focusing on dreams, not aspirations, as I understand the latter to imply a concrete approach to realising them, while dreams may rather serve as a motivator to continue and stabilise precarious lives.

When attempting to socially participate on platforms of visibility, reserved for the 'fortunate ones' with access to security measures, health support, social and physical mobility due to their status as a citizen or to their wealth, 'dream on!' is often the dismissive response, even if not necessarily in those words. As Scott put it: 'You can't sit with UCT[10] people if you're not a UCT member. I can go to UCT, but I don't have anything to say about science, economy, geography or sociology.'

Due to a lack of social capital, offering visibility, audibility and concrete tools for the carving away of obstacles, the act of aspiring is rendered difficult for many refugees. While there may be no physical hindrance to accessing spaces that signify privilege, body politics strategically exclude the poor and powerless at large. For male refugees engaging in various survival strategies, amongst which being sex work with predominantly male clients, the seemingly simple act of aspiring is further complicated by having to shift between life

---

[10] The University of Cape Town, arguably the most esteemed university in the Western Cape.

worlds that are likely to clash with ambiguous expectations and ideals – of work and private life, of life in Cape Town and the society into which they were born. Boundaries may sometimes be blurry and not easy to pinpoint but do require the ability to shift and negotiate in attempts to avoid risky situations. As Gupta and Ferguson (1997) have argued it in the context of refugees and their relationships with places and power structures, memory itself is exiled and shaken lose as its physical embodiments are erased. Imaginative uses of memory enable people, removed from their place of origin, to construct localities and communities as well as hybridised identities. Dreaming does not only incorporate the ability to imagine as a 'basis for the sustainable reproduction of cultural identities in the new society' (Appadurai, 2003:23) but, furthermore, offers a much broader basis for the men to resolve the multiple tensions of everyday life and to perform as an agent in fabricating them into something liveable, communal, respectable and, perhaps, comfortable.

Cities, like nations, have been argued to 'keep their shape by moulding their citizens' Sanderock (2003:33). In Cape Town, refugee men, I have argued in the previous chapters, often become moulded into 'disposable labourers' (Standing, 2011) with their bodies being deprived of any idealistic value. At the same time, movements between different spaces influence the process of re-making oneself. The men's corporeality is continuously re-made and undone, depending on the space, the different meanings the male refugee body is attributed in it and the kinds of socialites that thus become possible within. In negotiating ambiguous and sometimes conflicting meanings of their body-selves, the men become exposed to processes of change and rupture, evolving around experiences and understandings of time, space, self, body and identity (Van Wolputte, 2004). I am arguing that the fragmentation of a body-self along various axes, such as past and present or public and private, and the sometimes violent rupture between experience and discourse (see Van Wolputte, 2004) can, to some degree, be overcome in the act of dreaming.

Thus, dreams can be seen as a way of achieving a sense of belonging, as they offer a form of engagement with the discrepancy between a structurally undermined self on the one hand, and the meanings attached to the men's body-selves as negotiated in different societal spaces on the other. In the following section, I will show how, through the practice of dreaming, memory and imagination may reconcile conflicting images of the self in their interplay.

I will look at the men's descriptions of a possible future as what Hollan (2004) has conceptually framed as selfscape dreams. According to Hollan (2004), dreams provide a map of the self's contours in the present in resonance with the engagement of the body with other objects and people in the world, across spaces and at different points in time. In my spending time with male refugees, I regarded both biological and imaginative processes to be highly relevant. Engagements with the world take place on multiple levels for the men, in the past as well as in the present and future and desires, fuelled by imagination, constitute a person the same way physical experience does. What is more, subconscious desires might affect actions in various ways (Hollan, 2004) and thus powerfully find their expression in life histories, as will become evident throughout the rest of this chapter.

Challenging vulnerability through stability

Issa invited me to meet him at the UCT medical school

where he was working for a few months. While making our way through the uniformly beige passageways, I struggled to keep up with his pace. His tall presence, his upright posture and apparent comfort in his movements stand out in this clinically neutral setting. The swiping of his access card became a symbolic act of pride, as though offering a form of compensation for the disappointments and insecurities not just of his past but also ongoing experiences outside these walls of privilege. When entering the cafeteria, round in shape and surrounded by glass, Issa started chatting away loudly, despite the spiralling of his voice through the silence. In the stories shared by him, multiple and intersecting factors of precarity and precariousness (Butler, 2016) affecting his life came to the fore, as did the ways in which he strategically and imaginatively engaged with them. Through his narrative, it also became clear how some aspects of insecurity have become building stones for a particular version of self.

Openly identifying as 'gay' and being from Rwanda, Issa was still considering whether to 'come out' to his parents with his sexual preference as he worried about their response. He considered the stigma attached to men having relationships with other men to be embodied in his home country. There was a grin on his face when he described how he used to dress up in his mother's clothes as a child and how, when he was older, his mother used to say that he was meant to be born as a woman. Their neighbours openly interpreted his long dreadlocks as a signifier for his homosexuality. The love his family members have for one another, Issa calls 'soul love' and he is certain that they know about his homosexual identity by now, with his brother having indicated that they tolerate it quietly. However, he was still worried about facing his family's judgement when actually having an open conversation about this. Issa also worried about getting older and retiring from sex work permanently:

> 'I'm getting tired. I don't feel like I'll continue to do the sex work. But, you know, this is something which you can't run away from. Because it is not something you learn at school. It is something we have' (Issa, SWEAT, 17th of June 2014).

In other words, he had embodied being what he understands to be a 'sex worker'. Issa actively approached his retirement by establishing contacts with different organisations. He was volunteering at Health4Men (whose agenda it is to educate men about health-related issues), and at a HIV- related trial at the UCT medical school. Via his volunteering efforts at UCT and an unpaid internship that followed, he made it onto the payroll of the trial as a fieldworker in informal settlements. It was his responsibility to introduce HIV-prevention methods and collect feedback from participants, something he described as very straining and difficult, as many of the participants struggle with addiction, were unreliable or difficult to get hold of. However, he felt comfortable in the position to educate and described this as his 'mission', particularly with regards to homosexuality. Issa proudly told me that he had been part of a documentary about stigmata related to homosexuality (through STEPS, another organisation with which he is affiliated and which produces documentaries) and said he was wishing for the ability to stream it for other refugees, whom he felt the most stigmatised by as a man openly referring to himself as gay. Other insecurities he was facing on a daily basis, especially in the settlement Delft where he lived, Issa considered to be perpetuated by uncaring structures and institutions:

'The government in South Africa does not see a refugee in terms of ... this refugee needs help from the government. You know, a refugee who left doesn't even have an ID, doesn't even have clothes to wear, doesn't even have underwear or slippers. But you can't see the government helping this kind of person. Even getting that paper, it's a problem. [...] It's government leaders. If they went to say to people "imagine it was you ..." I'm sure people can change and everything would be fine [...] People need to be educated. But now people only get a hate-crime message.' (Issa, SWEAT, 17th of June 2014)

Issa has been struggling to establish meaningful relationships built on trust in South Africa and wishes for a partner whom he can rely on and who will stand by him in difficult times. In the past, two of his partners drastically turned against him after an argument and one threatened to report him to the police as a rapist. He considered himself to be lucky to have been able to speak to a 'coloured woman' at the police station at the time so that he could clarify the situation, the outcome of which he suspected to have been different had he spoken to a 'black man'. Issa described these situations as highly stressful and unsettling - because he had to fear being deported but also because his trust was repeatedly betrayed. Having experienced the genocide and its aftermath in Rwanda as a young man and son of a politically active man and having come to South Africa as a refugee, caution has become a familiar companion. Being 38 years old, having relied on sex work as his primary income for years and attracting stigma as a foreigner and openly homosexual man, Issa worries about being able to have a stable relationship some day:

'My vision was to get someone stable whereby we can even get married. It's not easy … to trust those guys with all those decisions I made, with the travels I had … I don't feel safe. It's better now to leave it and when the time will come, maybe from nowhere it will happen' (Issa, cafeteria at UCT medical school, 3rd of June 2014).

In ensuring that his family accepts him the way he is, he described an imagine of him, one day, going to Rwanda with a fiancé and breaking the news of their engagement to be married to his family. The intersecting factors of age, sexual identification, his life as a sex worker and his status as a refugee in South Africa as well as the expectations linked to being a Rwandan man create a precarious matrix (see Collins, 2007) of everyday experiences in Cape Town, within which Issa imaginatively managed to negotiate conflicting aspects of his sense of self. In his narration, his body- self can be seen to shift in different spaces. In Rwanda, Issa tried to adhere to the expectations he was confronted with as a man. He got married and had three children with his wife but found male lovers on the side. However, he wanted his life to be different and moved to South Africa as he had read that homosexual marriages are legal there. Issa describes his first encounter with a client in Cape Town, an American man, and his own astonishment as the clients said that he would want to marry him, even though he knew about this being a legal possibility. Being able to declare that he identifies as homosexual means freedom to him, even if this 'freedom' comes with stigma in addition to the issues he faces as a refugee. Imagining himself permanently in the role of an educator, a role in which he feels respected and taken seriously, as well as in a stable relationship with a man who offers him continuous emotional support, hold the promise to reconcile his objectification as a refugee and as a man identifying as homosexual, on the one hand, and his shifting, fragmented corporeal experiences, on the other.

Issa's experiences and encounters very much depended on the context. The selves embodied at the UCT medical school or at the organisations he volunteers at are different from the ones embodied in informal settlements. When writing the introductory paragraphs to 'Issa's story', I remembered my first meeting with him and interviewing him right away in a stuffy storage room at SWEAT, filled with furniture that had been rescued from being painted along with the walls in the big meeting space. We arranged a couple of chairs and I watched the sun rays making the dust particles in the air dance, while Issa took charge of the recorder, holding it in his left hand while, every now and then, gesturing broadly with the other and thus punctuating his story. Our meetings were a way for him to take charge in telling stories of the past and presence and possible future. In ensuring access to particular institutions and outlets, Issa created a background against which he could dreamscape himself into a person experiencing respect, love and support, and thus agentively resisted oppressive hetero-normative ideals and other forms of oppression by using his imagination.

Imaginative resistance to limitations

Scott considered education to be a potential means to ultimately become rich. When encouraged to outline his future, he explained wanting to attend a school that a one-time client of his from overseas had told him about. As a control manager for rockets at the NASA, Scott explained, this client had more money than he could possibly spend. Asked what he would do with all this money, he replied that he would buy the biggest mansion imaginable and make investments to let his money produce more money. However, Scott does not expect this fairytale to simply emerge, but reasons that, initially, a rich customer might be able to help him finance school. He considers this unlikely but possible. His friend, he claims, was offered to get married to a wealthy European customer, accepted the proposal and moved with the man overseas, where Scott imagines him to live rather comfortably. 'Maybe somebody will ask me to marry him,' he said to me with a smile on his face.

Scott frequently re-affirmed his heterosexual identity throughout our conversations. However, he also described enjoyment when having sex with men and would sometimes have oral sex with men 'for fun' (as opposed to 'doing business'). He also showed interest in regulations in 'Europe' in terms of same-sex relationship as well as sex work. Having a transgendered girlfriend and exclusively male clients is, to him, not comparable with mindsets and practices of whom he dismissingly calls 'the gays'. Leaning uncomfortably closely in, Scott mentioned to me that he is 'still' paying for sex with women but should get married at some point, once his life has changed, as this is his obligation as a 'man'. This constituted an abrupt shift from a rather relaxed conversation about his daily routines, causing me to think about myself as a platform for Scott to perform the hetero-normative ideals he has internalised.

Scott moved back and forth from Delft almost every day and the self-embodied in the settlement differed from the one that became possible in the park in the city centre, where business and leisure, enjoyment and necessity form a symbiosis. While, in his home in Delft, he made sure not to attract too much attention, the park offered him the freedom to converse with different people and to be more at ease. The way he experienced the space impacted on his notion of self and vice versa. He knew well enough how to circumvent unpleasant surprises in the park – something that was not possible in Delft, where his movements were restricted and linked to specific times in the interest of his safety. The different social encounters he had in the park, whether it was escorting clients to the toilets, spending time with his girlfriend or exchanging thoughts with people whom he identified as fellow sex workers, required negotiation, fragmenting the self in accordance with different desires (love, money, and sociality).

The various meanings attached to his body-self had to be re-negotiated in different circumstances but became somewhat reconciled in the park, where vital movements continue even throughout winter time. Here, tourists encounter the shelterless and sex workers who may settle down just a few metres away from women with prams, out on a leisurely stroll. The security guards, Scott said, let people be, as long one does not act suspiciously, meaning that there are no indicators for illegal activities such as sex work or drug consumption. He avoided falling asleep though as to be on his toes and to convey that he was inhabiting the space only transitionally. For Scott, the space carried a potential for radical change for the better and the possibility to take on different identities. Scott's imaginative marriage to a rich man was described as offering possible security and financial ease, enabling him to pursue other dreams and opening up opportunities to explore himself in contexts in which he may not be dismissingly labelled 'gay'. In his self-scape dreams, Scott found himself in a relationship and embarking upon a future that promising all kinds of possibilities – class mobility, moving beyond gender categories as well as physical borders into a fantastic land associated with freedom.

Daniel's idea of such free movement went beyond just 'making it' overseas. He told me about an international refugee passport he wanted to obtain, which would enable him to become a 'citizen of the world' and travel anywhere freely. The idea of a 'citizen of the world' not only transcends borders and notions of 'insiders and outsiders' (Nyamnjoh, 2006) but also dualisms of the body and mind. Knowing that one is welcome anywhere in the world and not seen as an outsider anymore, taking up space and opportunities in the crowded cities of the world, would render the actual travel unnecessary. Daniel also told me about his cousin who had met his wife in Germany and had taken her back to his home country Mozambique, adding that, where he is from, 'mixed couples' are rather ordinary. His dream-scaped self was neither confined to physical borders, nor to racial or social ones. Daniel's suggestion that it just takes a regulatory change to create a scenario in which his presence would be perceived very differently was underlined by using my body (associated with being from Germany, being socially flexible and mobile) as a contrast in pointing out the absurdity of his predicament.

Imagination as healing practice and inspiration to keep on dreaming

Miguel met his father for the first time when he arrived in Port Elizabeth by himself as a 19-year-old. In Mozambique, he used to live with his grandparents. His mother worked at the airport and was out of the country most of the time. Nevertheless, he said, she would always spoil him upon her return. Although he felt love from the rest of his family, he picked up that they did not approve of his mother remaining unmarried and missing out on giving her son important life lessons due to being away and not having a father figure in the house. When Miguel grew up, he learnt that his father was a panel beater and now lived in South Africa so he decided to move countries and explore the kinship ties that he considered himself more connected to than the ones from his mother's side of the family as he made repeatedly clear by saying 'my surname if from my father' and 'I don't belong in that surname [of the mother]'.

Before his arrival in Port Elizabeth, Miguel had imagined what it would be like working side by side with his father in the latter's panel beating shop and maybe getting his own car, in which he could proudly return to his home town for a visit: 'They tell me all these things. He's nice, he can give me a job, he has two cars. My life can change, I can be ... you see. [...] When I left from Mozambique and came here I told all my friends I'm gonna change. I'm gonna have a car ... and I can come there.' This vision of exploring his kinship ties is linked to the adventure of seeking greener pastures abroad which, in turn, is tied to expectations of accumulating wealth (see Tazanu, 2012). Yet, things turned out differently. His father, who had left for work in South Africa before he was born had never come back to visit, but was reportedly in an intact relationship with Miguel's mother. However, Miguel discovered that his father lived with a wife and his two daughters in South Africa, the oldest of whom was five years younger than Miguel. His father's Setswana-speaking wife had no idea that he had a son; neither did she know that her husband was originally from Mozambique, as he had learnt to speak Setswana fluently and without an accent. His father's wife, who Miguel referred to as his step-mother, despised his presence and made this clear by denying him food from the 'same pot' as her family. He realised that his father would not defend him, was hardly at home and, when he was around, he would be drunk. After yet another conflict with his stepmother, Miguel took off without having anywhere to go. He stayed outdoors in Port Elisabeth and delivered newspapers for R1200 per month before catching a train to Cape Town, where he was hoping to find a better job. When asked why he did not return to Mozambique when things turned out so disappointingly, he replied that he could not have done so without having something to show upon his return: 'I only go if there's something ... if I bring myself up and I'm not dependent'. His mother had been pushing him to reveal to her where he was so that she could visit, which had led him to restrain himself from contacting her for half a year out of a feeling of embarrassment for his situation. 'Me, if I die here,' he says, 'I can't explain to my mother.' He expressed concern about his mother finding out 'the truth' about his life with him being her only child and her then insisting on him coming back to Mozambique without having improved himself. Lying to her and avoiding her places a burden upon him:

> 'They tell me all these things. He's nice, he can give me a job, he has two cars. My life can change, I can be ... you see. [...] When I left from Mozambique and came here I told all my friends I'm gonna change. I'm gonna have a car ... and I can come there.' (Miguel, Park in Observatory, 19th of June 2014)

Miguel did not see any way out of his situation but was hoping to be able to afford a room or flat one day. In order to be able to transport an image of himself back to Mozambique in line with his dream-scaped self, he had a picture of himself taken in front of a house in Sea Point in borrowed clothes. This story reminded me of Gondola's (1999) description of Congolese youth, who, having moved to European metropolises such as Paris, create spaces for a dreamlike 'reincarnation' (see the Freudian concept of dreaming) in the wake of harsh realities faced as African foreigners. Using designer clothes, which they manage to access in spite of meagre salaries, these young people create a glamorous illusion and validate their quest for a new sense of self. Miguel and the other men I spent time with did not have access to stable jobs and even if they were to get access to fancy clothing, they would struggle to remain in possession of them. However, the men did dress with care and their appearance is usually neat, even if there was nothing standing out in the way they dressed. A reincarnation or dream-scaping, due to the scarcity of resources, thus largely unfolded in reliance on the men's imaginative capacities.

It was Miguel's wish to, one day, return to Mozambique and be able to 'spoil my madre and myself'. The last time I saw Miguel, he told me excitedly that he had managed to get a new passport (the last one had been stolen with the rest of his possessions) and that he could get better work now that it was also slowly getting warmer. He mused about saving money and thereby creating more stability in his life. Even though Miguel pointed out the positive aspects of his life and visions of a brighter future, his initial dream of being re-united with his father and starting a new life, crushed within one month of staying with him, left a deeply-seated pain that became audible through the cracks of his voice whenever he returned to the topic. In evaluation with his memories and his present and past relationships, Miguel's dream-scaped self was described by him as a reliable adult who overcomes the obstacles he is faced with independently and manages to take care of his family.

Fabrications of the self through dreams constitute a move away from the forcefully moulded 'denizen' (Standing, 2011) and open up worlds of possibilities. The realisation of these possibilities seemed pointless to proactively aspire to in the now or the immediate future, given the men's limited resources, lack of institutional access and reliance on networks that sometimes turned out to be brittle. Thus, notions of self are in a constant process of becoming – being moulded externally and re- moulded from within with themes such as manhood, kinship and meaningful relationships frequently re-occurring. Dream-scaped selves can be considered fuel that keeps the men going in the face of severe precarity, rendering life a little lighter in the cautious manoeuvring of the city. They can furthermore be seen as part of a 'hidden transcript' (Scott 1990) and thus as forms of resistance to oppressive structures.

After all, dream-scaped selves serve as an impediment to constant attacks on the bodily integrity of male refugees in Cape Town in that they offer an opportunity of re-defining themselves. The ability to mould the contours of the self constitutes an agentive act, which does, however, not necessarily have to translate onto concrete actions. There was not always a precise plan or pursuit to realise dreams as some things, for instance meeting someone 'special', cannot be actively orchestrated. I understand the dreams shared with me as having the powerful capacity to create meaning where there appeared to be a lack thereof. They furthermore created a sense of belonging and stability whilst being exposed to a push and pull of being objectified and becoming fragmented again. In this process, the dream-scaped self not only offered comfort through the promise of something better that is yet to come, but also became part of everyday corporeal experiences.

Chapter 7

Conclusion:
Counter-weighing accelerated instabilities

This ethnography has sought to engage with the strategies employed by refugee men from different African countries in surviving and stabilising their existence in Cape Town. Even though the men's lives and bodies were exposed to severe precarity and precariousness, the men would find ways to maintained them as something signifying worth and prospect.

I found the male refugee body to carry multiple and sometimes conflicting meanings and messages in the study context, such as being perceived as a societal threat (accused of stealing jobs and women, being suspected criminals) and being symbolically and spatially forced into the bottom ranks of society. However, they were also carriers of modes by which a better tomorrow and version of the self could be envisioned. These conflicts came through in various narratives and via different themes, such as the body ageing, the body in relationships, the body as a barrier, the body changing and longing and the body in other corporeal states of transformation. Bodies are never simply made but are in a state of becoming and can be undone in different ways and by different forces. Male refugees occupy different body-selves in different contexts and shift between spaces, in many of which they are objectified as less than human, while in others, a transcendence of this objectification becomes possible - at least to some degree. Imagination and corporeal experience, present and past, memory and vision are transformed in the process of occupying and navigating hostility in the Mother City carefully and strategically but also in stringing along joy and hope.

This ethnographic contribution is done in the hope that discursive regimes in South Africa and beyond will move towards a more intense engagement with the contemporary phenomenon of extensive migration, as the societal integration of refugees constitutes a necessity in a world in which 65 million refugees have become the new 'normal' rather than a state of emergency. This renders further insights into how people become part of new environments in spite of widespread hostility towards them crucial. In illuminating the social spheres that I have described as partially 'invisibilised' or camouflaged as public, 'unused' space, the negative associations linked to being a refugee (re-enforced by South African politicians as well as local media and police practices) and their pervasive influence on cultural imperatives will hopefully start becoming empirically diluted with an acknowledgement of the hopes, joys, skills, relationships and struggles of people on the move.

In a globalising context in which the gap between the rich and the poor increases alongside accelerated movements of people and ideas, a city like Cape Town, owing its attractiveness to being known as a place of beauty, affluence and opportunities, constitutes an interesting nexus and access point for future research to explore the experiences and intricacies of being categorised as a refugee (and thus an inherent outsider) onwards. However, research should extend beyond this South Africa and look at experiences in other African cities as well. I urge for a further excavation of the socialites that become possible in the sometimes camouflaged niches that refugees are forced to inhabit, as this will shed some light on the purposefully shadowed relationships of the precariat (Sharp, 2008; Standing, 2011).

Bibliography

Aggleton, P. ed., 1999. *Men who sell sex: International perspectives on male prostitution and HIV/AIDS*. Temple University Press.

Allison, A., 2012. 'Ordinary refugees: Social precarity and soul in 21st century Japan'. *Anthropological Quarterly*, 85(2), 345-370.

Appadurai, A., 2003. 'Archive and aspiration'. *Information is Alive*. Rotterdam: V2 Publishing.

Bernard, H.R., 1998. Introduction. On Method and Methods in Anthropology, in HR Bernard. *Handbook of Methods in Cultural Anthropology*. London: Alta Mira, 9-14.

Bernard, H.R., and Bernard, H.R., 2013. *Social Research Methods: Qualitative and Quantitative Approaches*. London: Sage.

Biehl, J., 2007. 'Ex-human reflections on Vita: Life in a zone of social abandonment'. *City & Society*, 19(1), 81-85.

Bourdieu, P., 1986. The forms of capital. *Handbook of Theory and Research for the Sociology of Education*, 241-258.

Bourdieu, P., 1990. *Structures, habitus, practices*. Cambridge: Polity Press, 52-65.

Braudel, F., 1958. Histoire et sciences sociales: La longue durée. In *Annales. Histoire, Sciences Sociales*, 13(4), 725–753.

Brown, B., Duby, Z. and Bekker, L.G., 2012. Sex Workers. *An Introductory Manual for Health Care Workers in South Africa. 1st ed. Cape Town: Desmond Tutu HIV Foundation*.

Butler, J., 2016. *Frames of war: When is life grievable?*. Verso Books.

Chabal, P., 2009. *Africa: The Politics of Suffering and Smiling*. London: Zed Books.

Marcus, G.E., 1986. Afterword: ethnographic writing and anthropological careers. *Writing culture: The poetics and politics of ethnography*, pp.262-6.

Clifford, J., 1988. *The predicament of culture*. Harvard University Press.

Collins, P., 2007. *Intersecting Oppressions*. Available at: www.uk.sagepub.com/.../13299_Chapter_16_Web_Byte _Patricia_Hill_Collins_PDF (accessed on the 13th of May 2014).

Collins, P. and Gallinat, A. eds., 2013. *The ethnographic self as resource: Writing memory and experience into ethnography*. Berghahn Books.

Cornwall, A., 2000. Missing men? Reflections on men, masculinities and gender in GAD. *IDS Bulletin*, 31(2), 18-27.

Crush, J. and Tawodzera, G., 2014. Medical xenophobia and Zimbabwean migrant access to public health services in South Africa. *Journal of Ethnic and Migration Studies*, 40(4), 655-670.

Csordas, T.J. ed., 1994. *Embodiment and experience: The existential ground of culture and self* (Vol. 2). Cambridge University Press.

Csordas, T., 1999. Embodiment and cultural phenomenology. *Perspectives on Embodiment: The Intersections of Nature and Culture*, 143-162.

De Certeau, M., 2004. "Making do": Uses and tactics. *Practicing History: New Directions in Historical Writing After the Linguistic Turn*, New York: Routledge.

Emirbayer, M. and Mische, A., 1998. 'What is agency?' *American Journal of Sociology* 103(4), 962- 1023.

Geertz, C., 1973. Thick description: Toward an interpretive theory of culture. *The Interpretation of Cultures: Selected Essays*. New York: Basic Books, 3-30.

Gondola, D., 1999. Dream and drama: The search for elegance among Congolese youth. *African Studies Review*, 42(1), 23-

48.

Gordon, S.L., 2016. Welcoming refugees in the rainbow nation: contemporary attitudes towards refugees in South Africa. *African Geographical Review*, *35*(1), 1-17.

Gorven, A.R., 2014. Sex Workers' Discursive Constructions of Intimate Partner Violence.

Gupta, A. and Ferguson, J., 1997. Discipline and practice: 'The field' as site, method, and location in anthropology. *Anthropological locations: Boundaries and grounds of a field science*, *100*, 1-47.

Gutmann, M.C., 1997. Trafficking in men: The anthropology of masculinity. *Annual Review of Anthropology*, 26, 385–409.

Harris, B., 2002. Xenophobia: A new pathology for a new South Africa. *Psychopathology and social prejudice*, 169-184.

Hollan, D., 2004. The anthropology of dreaming: Selfscape dreams. *Dreaming*, *14*(2-3), 170-182.

Idemudia, E.S., 2017. Trauma and PTSS of Zimbabwean refugees in South Africa: A summary of published studies. *Psychological trauma: theory, research, practice, and policy*, *9*(3), 252.

Jensen, S., 2008. *Gangs, politics & dignity in Cape Town.* James Curey Ltd.

Jewkes, R., Morrell, R., Sikweyiya, Y., Dunkle, K. and Penn-Kekana, L. 2012. Transactional relationships and sex with a woman in prostitution: prevalence and patterns in a representative sample of South African men. Bio Med Central, 12, 325.

Lock, M., 1993. Cultivating the body: Anthropology and epistemologies of bodily practice and knowledge. *Annual Review of Anthropology*, 22, 133-155.

Lévi-Strauss, C., 1966. The savage mind, Chicago (The University of Chicago Press) 1966.

Mamabolo, L.L., 2017. *Exploring resilience among female sex workers in Johannesburg* (Doctoral dissertation).

Marcus, G.E., 1995. Ethnography in/of the world system: The emergence of multi-sited ethnography. *Annual review of anthropology*, *24*(1), 95-117.

Mbembe, A., 1992. 'Prosaics of servitude and authoritarian civilities'. *Public culture*, *5*(1), 123-145.

Mpe, P., 2001. *Welcome to our Hillbrow*. Pietermaritzburg: University of Natal Press.

Massawe, D., and Kueppers, C., 2010. Sex Work Research and Advocacy: Research as a Means to Empower and Advance the Rights of Sex Workers.

Ndjio, B., 2006. *Feymania: New wealth, magic money and power in contemporary Cameroon*. PhD dissertation, University of Amsterdam.

Ndjio, B., 2008. Cameroonian feymen and Nigerian '419' scammers: Two examples of Africa's reinvention of the global capitalism. African Studies Centre Leiden Working Paper.

Nyamnjoh, F., 2006. *Insiders and outsiders: Citizenship and Xenophobia in Contemporary Southern Africa*. London: Zed Books.

Obrist, B., 2006. *Struggling for Health in the City: An Anthropological Inquiry of Health, Vulnerability and Resilience in Dar es Salaam, Tanzania*. Bern: Peter Lang.

Oliver, M.B., 2003. African-American men as "criminal and dangerous": Implications of media portrayals of crime on the "criminalization" of African American men. *Journal of African American Studies*, *7*(2), 3-18.

Pauw, I. and Brener, L., 2003. 'You are just whores—you can't be raped': barriers to safer sex practices among women street sex workers in Cape Town. *Culture, health &*